Amish Life

JOHN A. HOSTETLER

Herald Press

SCOTTDALE, PENNSYLVANIA / KITCHENER, ONTARIO

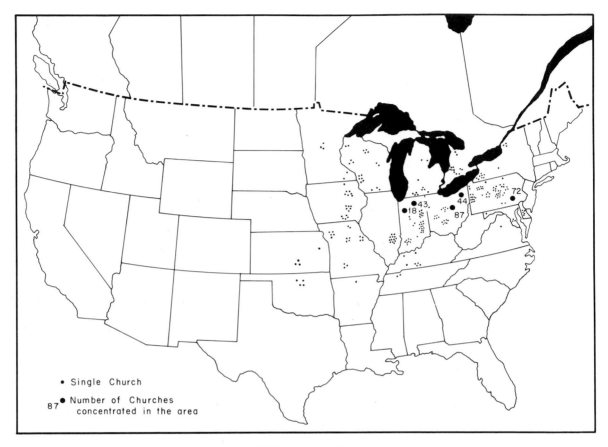

• Single Church

87 ● Number of Churches
concentrated in the area

Location of Old Order Amish communities,
United States and Canada.

AMISH LIFE, copyright © 1983 by Herald Press, Scottdale, Pa. 15683
Published simultaneously in Canada by Herald Press, Kitchener, Ont. N2G 4M5
Library of Congress Catalog Card Number: 82-83964
International Standard Book Number: 0-8361-3326-9
Printed in the United States of America
Design by Sue Bishop
83 84 85 86 87 10 9 8 7 6 5 4 3 2 1

A Little Commonwealth

The Amish people are neither relics of a bygone era nor a people misplaced in time. They have reached conclusions different from most moderns about how to live in today's world. Their past is alive in their present. They are living examples of a different form of modernity.

Industralized societies have not absorbed the Amish people in the same way that many subcultures have been assimilated. The experts predicted that the Amish would be assimilated into the dominant society once the vitality of their European customs was exhausted. But the experts were wrong. The Amish population has doubled in the past twenty-five years. Their communities are distinctive and viable.

Although the Amish are often featured in newspapers and magazines, research journals, books, and pamphlets, many misconceptions still persist. On the one hand, the Amish are viewed as a rare species, a people who live "naturally" and who approximate the requirements of sainthood. On the other extreme are those who pity the Amish for not accepting the most modern conveniences and for not asserting their individual rights as taken for granted by most Americans.

The Amish people did not originate in a corporate board meeting but in the suffering and martyrdom of the sixteenth century. The Amish are a church-community, a community whose members practice simple and austere living, a conservative branch of Christianity, a family-oriented labor-intensive economic system. Their present life is still shaped by the faith and struggle of their European past. In some respects the Amish are a little commonwealth, for their members are ruled by the law of love and redemption. They are highly sensitive to each other's needs. They will move to other lands rather than take up arms or defend themselves.

A Redemptive Community

The Amish view themselves as a *Gemeinde,* a corporate community, where the ethical teachings of Jesus are practiced. The love of God requires an appropriate response. The Amish do not believe that doing good deeds will get them to heaven, yet without such attributes they believe ultimate meaning is impossible.

The Amish were among the early Germanic settlers in William Penn's woods, or Pennsylvania. They originated in the Anabaptist movement (1525–1536) which gave rise to several Christian communities that survive to this day: the Mennonites of the Netherlands, the Hutterites of Austria, and the Swiss Brethren. The Amish are a branch of the Swiss group, taking their name from Elder Jacob Ammann (in 1697), who stood for conserving traditions and separation from the world to a greater extent than other Anabaptist groups.

All Anabaptist groups suffered martyrdom for their deviation from the established Catholic, Lutheran, or Reformed churches. From a renewed study of the Bible, they held that membership in the Christian church should be voluntary (adult instead of infant baptism), that church and state should be separate, that believers are required to practice the teaching and example of Christ in a disciplined community. Their reforms were greeted with deportation and death. They suffered as heretics at the hand of church and state, being burned at the stake and tied to wagon wheels. Many were placed in sacks and thrown into the river or tortured in other cruel ways as described in their book of martyrs.

The Amish are a "community people." Their understanding of the Bible requires them to live in a redemptive community. Like most Christians, the Amish believe in the authority of the Bible. They do not, however, emphasize individualistic conversion to the exclusion of community. Today's (Swiss Mennonites) come from the same seventeenth-century stock as the Amish, but they differ in the degree of modernization. The Amish have incorporated more of the past into

Replenishing the lanterns with kerosene
is one of the weekly cleaning duties.

A Lancaster County, Pennsylvania, farm. Farms are owned
and operated by the family.

their communities—in their manner of worship, simplicity, styles of dress, and high degree of nonverbal and symbolic communication. They cherish personal relationships over organizational relationships, and they maintain restraints on modern technology. The Amish meet for worship in their homes. They avoid higher education, do not conduct missionary work, nor do they install electricity or telephones in their homes.

The Amish View of Other Anabaptists

To a remarkable degree the Amish people are not judgmental of outsiders or of persons of another faith. They do not feel compelled to convert others to their way of life. The Mennonites see this as a deterioration of the faith or neglect of duty. Their relationship to their parental group, the Mennonites, may be characterized as a love-hate relationship.

Ever since the Amish-Mennonite division in the late seventeenth century, the Amish have regarded the Mennonites as more worldly than themselves. However, when Amish members modernize their homes or buy an automobile they typically join a Mennonite-related group. Because Mennonites teach the Anabaptist faith (including nonresistance), their churches are less objectionable to the Amish than more worldly churches. In time of war or national crisis, the Amish and the Mennonites cooperate in maintaining conscientious objector status and in responding to the needs of refugees and war-stricken people.

From the viewpoint of the Amish, today's Mennonites participate too fully in modern society. With the acceptance of higher education and the bureaucratic organizational patterns—the formation of conferences, boards, committees, and their busyness with activities, missionary work, welfare, education, and service programs—the Mennonites have lost the quality of their communities and their children to the ends of the earth.

There is an invisible line the Old Order Amish will not cross. The Amish live within highly personalized relationships, in neighborhoods, extended family groups, and communities, with major portions of their lives controlled by their folkways. When they become "educated," whether through Mennonite or "English" ways, they cross that invisible line. The threshold is marked by association with whole categories of strangers, indiscriminate exposure to the world, rationality rather than intuition, verbalization of religious experience, and fragmentation rather than integration.

Survival in America

The Amish have completely disappeared from their European homeland. Considered heretics, they could not own land in Europe, and those who did not emigrate were absorbed into other churches. Ironically, they have survived in America, supposedly the "melting pot" of the world.

Today Amish communities exist in twenty states and in the province of Ontario. Three-fourths of the Amish live in the states of Pennsylvania, Ohio, and Indiana. The Amish do not live in isolated colonies, villages, or compounds. They are scattered throughout the countryside, around small rural towns, and interspersed among "English" (non-Amish) farm families. The Amish are not a commune nor a monastic order, not a social class or caste, but a religious community constituting a subculture in America. As a corporate group wherever they live, they represent a community of "one mind," one discipline, and "one body."

During the eighteenth century with other Germanic-speaking people, the Amish came to America. They first settled in Berks, Chester, and Lancaster counties in southeastern Pennsylvania. The first ship to carry persons with typical Amish names was *The Adventure,* sailing from Rotterdam and arriving in Philadelphia on October 2, 1727. It is likely that a few Amish families arrived in

Houses built by the Amish about two centuries ago
in Alsace, France, are still standing.

Family carriage of the conservative
whitetop Amish.

America before that time but the records are lacking. They first began to move from Pennsylvania to Ohio in 1808, to Indiana in 1839, and to Iowa in 1846.

The Amish have large families, a low rate of infant mortality, and prohibitions against birth control. Like other Americans they also tend to live longer than in years past. They have experienced a much greater net population gain in recent decades than have non-Amish populations. The rate of childlessness among Amish couples is lower than that for the United States population as a whole. The average number of live births per family is seven. In 1980, Amish congregations numbered 550 and the total population was about 88,000. Ohio has more Amish than any other state in the union, followed by Pennsylvania and Indiana. Despite the number of Amish children who do not join the church of their parents, or who leave and become "English," the Amish are not threatened by a decline in membership.

Agriculture

The Amishman does not farm because it promises the shortest route to financial rewards. On the contrary, he works with his hands and saves so that he can eventually buy a farm and raise his family in a redemptive community. The Amish way of life requires members to make their living from the soil or from farm-related activities.

The account of creation and the parables in the Bible inform the Amishman that he must be a steward of the soil. He is to till and care for the soil with his labor and oversight. If the land is treated violently or exploited, it will yield poorly, leaving mankind in poverty. The Amish believe that with good management the land will not only yield a livelihood, but as in the Garden of Eden, their farms should reflect pleasantness and orderliness.

The Amish people enjoy a high reputation as good farmers, though in practice this quality is not uniformly found in all communities.

Lancaster County, Pennsylvania, has long been acclaimed "The Garden Spot" of the nation, not only because its soil is the most productive in the world, but because of sound management. No other Amish community today excels this area in outward appearance—in well-kept farm dwellings and fields, abundant gardens, and tidy children.

The Amish prefer to raise a diversity of crops and livestock rather than a single cash crop. They grow corn, oats, rye, several hay crops for feeding, and vegetables for home consumption. They feed the grain to their horses, dairy cattle, beef cattle, hogs, poultry, and sheep. Because of the high price of farmland and the diminishing size of their farms, some of the Amish have been forced to raise "cash" crops such as tomatoes, peas, potatoes, and tobacco. Most Amish farmers also maintain dairy herds and sell whole milk.

The ability to manage farms and to transform unproductive lands into fertile farms was acquired by the Amish in Europe. In Switzerland, Alsace, and Germany they excelled as farmers. Already in the seventeenth century they practiced rotation of crops, indoor feeding of livestock, meadow irrigation, use of animal fertilizer, and raised new varieties of clover as a means of restoring soil fertility. These productive practices have been effectively transmitted for generations.

Managing a farm, as understood by the Amish, requires a high degree of commitment by the husband, wife, and children. Children grow up helping both parents. Qualities which go into good management include a whole complex of attitudes: willingness to start the day early, working cooperatively with nature and with other family members, knowing how to include children in family labor, maintaining punctuality and orderliness, keeping tools in place and in good repair, maintaining good varieties of livestock and horses, learning to preserve food and conserve costs, and not shrinking from the requirements of hard work. Wives are frequently in close control of the flow of information and finances. Banks generally find that loans to the Amish are a sound investment, and mortgages are never foreclosed because of divorce.

Corn is harvested for dairy feed
by this Amish family.

Amish-Scale Technology

The Amish have long foreseen the dangers of ambitious technology or what the world calls "progress." For more than a century the Amish have been coping with the irresistible trend for units of production to become larger and larger. When tractor power overtook horse power in American agriculture, the Amish retained their horse-drawn equipment. When electricity was made available to rural people, the Amish stayed with their kerosene lanterns and gasoline-run engines. When small acreages were consolidated into large farms for commercial agriculture, the Amish preferred to keep their small farms.

The Amish are moderate consumers of energy. In many communities they use windmills. In Lancaster County, Pennsylvania, they often harness streams in their meadows by constructing waterwheels. In some regions water is piped from a natural spring or reservoir in the mountains. The Amish use less fuel, chemical fertilizer, feed, and modern equipment than do commercial farmers.

By holding large-scale technology at a distance, and by restraining its influence on their lives, they have managed to maintain the integrity of their family and community life. They will not let technology and efficiency run away with their family and community. The fascination with bigger and more efficient machines in worldly society contrasts sharply with the Amish practice of moderation and restraint. They have chosen social solidarity, and by doing so are one of the few societies in the world who are master over their machines.

The Amish accept some changes, but only after it has been demonstrated that the change will not erode the unity of their community. They mount small motors on horse-drawn farm equipment to operate the farm implements. They use small pocket calculators, felt-tip pens, and ball bearings on their buggy wheels. They adopt many of the inventions of the secular society once they are outmoded. By combining family labor with modest acreages, and by restraining the trend toward

14

A young Amish blacksmith and his farm shop.

large and costly machines, they have been able to escape some of the disintegrating aspects of modern society—haste, waste, aimlessness, and violence.

The Non-Farming Amish

Occupational patterns among the Amish have changed significantly since about 1960. Due to the scarcity and high cost of farmland, and the expensiveness of farm machinery and supplies, many of the younger Amish couples have been forced to work off the farm. During the past two decades those who did not wish to give up farming have formed new communities in other areas of Pennsylvania, in Missouri, Minnesota, Wisconsin, Iowa, and in Ontario.

Many of the non-farming Amish work in trades and shops within the Amish community as carpenters and cabinetmakers in the lumber and building trades. The new shops and services support the economic life of the agriculturally based community. The Amish are no longer dependent on the non-Amish for many services. They now operate appliance centers, engine shops, farm equipment and plow shops, harness shops, printshops, shoe stores, bookstores, and a variety of services such as watch repairing, locksmithing, and carriage-making. The shops and services, not advertised, are typically located on Amish farms. Some gardeners and farmers sell vegetables and produce to the public directly from their farms.

Amish people who are employed by non-Amish employers constitute a small percentage of the population in Lancaster County. In other areas the percentage is much higher. In northern Indiana many of the Amish work in small industries in rural areas, especially in mobile home and boat factories. Employment of this type is often viewed as a temporary means to save money toward the purchase of a farm. Since factory work separates parents from children, and the family from the land, this work is viewed with disfavor.

Garments are typically washed on Monday.

An Amish kitchen. The black propane stove
is fueled by bottled gas.

Children's play is combined with important family tasks.

The Family

The family, among the Amish, is marked by stability. The most important activity is child-rearing. The size of the church is measured in the number of families in a district. In marriage, husband and wife become "one flesh," a single unit dissolved only by death. Although the husband is "head of the wife," the wife is seen as having an immortal soul and not merely as an extension of her husband. She is given an equal vote in church, and decides whether she is prepared to take communion. Should her husband sin to the extent that he is placed under the "ban," she will join all the other members of her church in shunning him. The husband will do the same if his wife is put under the "ban."

An Amish woman knows what is expected of her. The home is her domain. Her duties include care of the children, cooking and cleaning, preparation of produce for market, preserving food for the family, gardening, and making clothes for each family member. The farm is the husband's kingdom, just as his wife is general manager of household affairs. Farms are typically owned jointly, and both partners may write checks and transact business at the bank.

Parents are careful to set a good example for the children. Harsh or boisterous talk between spouses is rare. Parents see themselves not only as mature adults respecting each other as persons, but as members of a kinship group and of the church whose standards they uphold. The birth of a child brings joy to the family and community, for children are wanted. The Amish home is an effective institution for training children so that they readily become socialized into the Amish way of life. The earliest years of life are typically happy ones. The young child receives much attention from both parents, from siblings and cousins, aunts, uncles, and grandparents.

Teaching children to work and accept responsibility is considered of utmost importance. The boy learns to feed the farm animals, gather the eggs, feed the calves, and drive the horses. The girl learns domestic

Amish country school. Children play softball
during recess periods.

skills by helping her mother with the cooking and housekeeping. In adolescence the child is often given a pet or farm animal. The fate of the animal is linked to the care and attention given to it by the owner. In this way the child learns the consequences of routine feeding, growth, birth, sterility, disease, death, or neglect.

Gathering around the family table is one of the most important routines in the home. Silent prayers with bowed heads before and after each meal is the rule. Conversation at the table is often muted, but when a member is absent from the table, for any reason, there is empathy and concern for that member. The topics of conversation help set the tone for work and motivation. Here also the young learn the norms of behavior from older children and from parents. The Amish work hard and eat well. Amish gardens are a good source of fresh vegetables.

Schools

Most Amish children attend Amish schools, though in a few rural areas some still attend public schools. A half century ago when one-room schoolhouses still dotted the countryside, all Amish children attended public schools. When wholesale consolidation of schools occurred (from about 1937 to 1954), the Amish built their own small country schools and staffed them with their own teachers. The Amish sensed that if their children attended large schools, away from an agricultural environment, and were taught by teachers they did not know, their communities would be undermined.

All Amish children attend elementary school through grade eight. Most pupils walk to school. Where distance is a factor the Amish parents hire a school bus to transport their children. They are opposed to accepting government subsidies for any type of school support. Each school is administered by a school board, and attendance records are carefully kept for state inspection. The school is funded by the patrons and by the church. School buildings have coal or wood stoves and no electricity. The schools are built to maximize natural lighting.

Amish teachers are selected by each of the school boards on the basis of their aptitude for teaching and their interest in children. They have no formal training beyond grade eight, but after three years of apprenticed teaching they are considered qualified. Teacher training is primarily informal and personal. In addition to mastering the content of the subject matter, a teacher must be an example to the children in religious faith, in steadfastness, in love of fellowman, and in behavior. Teachers attend local and statewide Amish teachers' meetings in their community to lend each other support and to give and receive advice.

In school the children learn English, including reading, grammar, spelling, and penmanship. In arithmetic they learn addition, subtraction, multiplication, decimals, division, percentages, ratios, volumes, and weights and measures. Amish committees assist in the selection of books. In some areas the local public school donates their old textbooks to the Amish who find them less objectionable than new texts. The Amish also publish many of their own textbooks which stress community values.

The school helps the child to become a part of his community and to remain within his community. The school emphasizes shared knowledge and the dignity of tradition rather than change. The Amish stress accuracy rather than speed, drill rather than variety, proper sequence rather than freedom of choice. The curriculum as well as the mottoes on the interior walls stress honesty, thrift, purity, love, and cooperation, but without a heavy religious vocabulary. A well-run school has the atmosphere of a well-ordered family. The older children help the younger, and the pupils encourage one another's good performance so that the whole class or school may do well.

Amish elementary schools support the values taught in the family and in the church. Although Amish children do not study religion in the classroom, they learn a great deal about living their religion. The parents teach their own children within the family but they do not teach religion to the children of other families. Personal relationships

Interior of an Amish school during the lunch hour.

An Amish "scholar."

between teacher and pupil, along with memorization and recitation, are considered necessary preparation for life now and for eternity. True education, according to the Amish, is the cultivation of humility, simple living, and resignation to the will of God. Like their forefathers, they fear the dangers of "pagan" or "worldly" philosophy associated with self-exaltation, pride of position, enjoyment of power, and the arts of war and violence.

Youth

From birth to death, a person in Amish society passes through a series of distinct age stages. The recognized stages are: (1) little children, (2) scholars, (3) young folks, (4) adults, and (5) old folks. In each stage the individual learns to respond in approved ways. With role expectations clearly defined, there is a high degree of security and personal trust among members.

Most young people look forward to leaving elementary school. They know that important work is awaiting them on the farm. A boy works on his father's farm until he is knowledgeable in all aspects of farm work. A girl learns how to manage the household activities. A boy or girl may work for another Amish family if their services are needed.

From adolescence to marriage, the young person chooses his own friends, and usually finds a "crowd" he enjoys being with. He may sample the world and then must decide whether to join the Amish church and whom to marry. Some testing of the boundaries is expected, for the person must discover for himself what it means to be Amish.

The typical age for courtship, called "running around," begins at sixteen for the boy and may begin earlier for the girl. The opportunity to meet a large number of young people occurs at the Sunday evening "singing," a gathering for the unmarried only. Who one courts is often a guarded secret, and although most parents know who is going with their child, it is not a subject for conversation. The young Amishman's choice of a wife is limited to a girl in the Amish church but not necessarily from his own community. The courtship may cover a span of several years, but in any case, baptism must occur before marriage.

Joining the Amish church generally takes place in the late teens or early twenties. Instruction in the faith is followed by baptism. Baptism signifies repentance, as well as commitment to the believing community and to its discipline. The Amish stress voluntary commitment, but once having vowed to become a member, there is no turning back. By breaking the vow of baptism one would invite excommunication and shunning.

The "New Birth"

Although the Amish church teaches spiritual "rebirth," the symbols of religious commitment are totally different from that of modern fundamentalist groups. The biblical passages are the same, but the interpretations are not.

The signs of spiritual rebirth, in sixteenth-century terms, are self-denial, submissiveness, obedience, and righteousness without flowery and embellished rhetoric. Emphasis is placed on the natural processes of growth and maturity such as partaking of the divine nature (2 Peter 1:4), being made heirs of the hope of salvation (Titus 3:5–7), and taking on the attributes and sufferings of Christ. The Amish emphasize repentance rather than soul-saving, and such personal experiences are typically quiet rather than dramatic. Amish conversions do not call attention to themselves.

Unlike most fundamentalist churches, the Amish emphasize submission to the corporate community of believers rather than personal liberation from sin. They stress cross-bearing and suffering rather than enjoyment, hope rather than assurance, a submissive attitude rather than a subjective experience, and above all a silent (nonverbal) expression of their faith rather than an outspoken testimony.

A group of girls in their Sunday dress.

The Amish meet in their farm homes for worship. Prior to the
event many women come to help prepare for the service.

An Amish barn raising may attract several hundred people.
The women prepare a hearty meal for the workers.

The spiritual ideals of the Amish are caught up in the German term *Gelassenheit* with its many meanings: resignation, calmness of mind, composure, staidness, conquest of selfishness, long-suffering, collectedness, silence of the soul, tranquility, inner surrender, yieldedness, equanimity, detachment, and residing quietly in Christ. Such attributes are believed to be acquired, not instantaneously at a specific time and place, but in a resolute walk through life in a redemptive community.

The Amish do not baptize their infants, nor worry about the salvation of their young souls. They believe that Christ's suffering and death was sufficient to atone for their children.

Marriage

A wedding is an elaborate affair, for the whole community has a stake in the marriage. Since weddings are the most important social events of the year and involve extensive preparations, most are scheduled after the fall harvest work is done. Ninety percent of all Amish marriages in Lancaster County, Pennsylvania, occur in November and December. They are celebrated on either a Tuesday or a Thursday.

In Amish life there is nothing comparable to formal engagement. When a couple decides to marry, the boy informs the deacon of his church who, as a go-between, obtains the consent of the girl's parents. The procedure is simply a formality. Following this, the bishop announces the intended marriage of the young couple in church. The wedding follows after a week or ten days. The first order of business for the groom is to personally invite all the relatives and friends to the wedding. Postcards are mailed to distant relatives.

The bride and groom wear new garments to their wedding, made in the same style as their best Sunday clothes. Blue is a typical color for a bride's dress. On the wedding day a regular church service is held which begins in the morning and ends at noon. The couple is attended by a bridal party of two unmarried couples, usually their own younger siblings. The bishop performs the marriage ceremony near the close of the service. After the formal service the invited guests are seated at tables for the wedding meal. The bridal party is seated at the "corner" which is loaded with special cakes and goodies. Following a festive meal, the rest of the day is spent singing and visiting into the late evening hours.

After an evening meal at the wedding tables, the older folks return to their homes while the young may stay until midnight, all the while visiting or playing wedding games. The wedding gifts of housewares and farm tools are displayed in one of the rooms for everyone to come and see. The couple spends their wedding night in the bride's home, and on the following day they help with the cleanup. Their "honeymoon" consists of visiting uncles, aunts, and friends for several weeks.

The parents of the newly married couple frequently take major responsibility for the economic establishment of the new home, particularly if they are a farm family. Long before the marriage, they may have prepared for the occasion by buying or renting another farm, or by building a "grandpa house" for themselves. They help provide furniture, livestock, and some of the basic necessities. Most newlyweds are given quilts and bedding by each of their mothers (and sometimes by their grandmothers). After moving into their new home the couple receives a great deal of help and social support from parents and friends.

The "Grandpa House"

Home is the center of life, a place of security, for all the family members. Most Amish children experience the closeness of another home, that of their grandparents. Many Amish farms have two dwellings, one of which is the smaller "grandpa house." At retirement

Many farm homes have large porches used for visiting,
and a second house called the "grandpa house."

31

Amish grandparents and their Mennonite grandchildren. Persons who leave the Amish tend to join related Anabaptist groups like the Mennonites.

from active duty the older couple moves into this house and typically a married son or daughter take over the main farmhouse.

A couple may voluntarily retire from farming at the age of fifty. By providing a farm for their children, the older couple will enhance their standing in the community. The Amish way of retiring is one of the soundest known. The old are not confronted with the choice between full-time work or no work at all. They work at will, as health and conditions permit, helping their married children become established on the farm. They may also work in small shops on the farm. They do not move to town, to an institution for the aged, nor do they accept welfare from the government.

The old folks live modestly. Though they may have paid for one or more farms in their lifetime, they are not typically wealthy by outside standards. By maintaining commonsense living arrangements, the values of old folks do not clash with those of the young couple. Even though they maintain intergenerational activity, each couple has independence of private housing and transportation. In community and church activities older men and women earn more respect with age. Wives have a significant influence in the extended family and on husbands who are leaders in the community. A retired couple can maintain customs and living arrangements they are comfortable with and have practiced all their life. Their house is sufficiently spacious to accommodate guests from a distance. They visit as well as receive many friends and relatives of all ages. Because they are not isolated and because they have an important status in the community, there is no problem of loneliness.

Most Amish have experienced years of physical labor. Bodily exercise has helped them to remain physically healthy and active in work as well as in community affairs such as frolics, auctions, weddings, and in making quilts, braided rugs, and wooden toys. Older folks continue their involvement in such activities. When sickness strikes, relatives and friends come to visit frequently. No stigma is attached to being sick. The Amish receive medical care from nearby physicians and from local hospitals.

Amish children enjoy skating on a farm pond.

Community Cohesion

The strength of the Amish community cannot be accounted for simply by the perpetuation of tradition. There are many social bonds—religious, historic, linguistic, economic, family, and kinship—in addition to personal commitment to the faith. Formal commitment signifies self-sacrifice, submission, obedience, right living, and caring, without lofty words and language. The commitment is made to God and the redemptive community, and its *Ordnung* (rules).

The Amish people meet in their homes for worship on Sunday. Each family attends the preaching services in its own district. The services are rotated among households, generally on an annual schedule. The three-hour services consist of singing, meditation, and preaching. Following a noon meal, the members visit and the children play for long periods with each other. Each congregation nominates, chooses by lot, and ordains its own leaders who serve for life.

Community cohesion is supported by the way in which the past is incorporated into the present. This is illustrated in the uses the Amish make of chanted music in worship and by their conversational speech. All Amish people, wherever they live, speak three distinctive tongues. Their household speech is a dialect called Pennsylvania German or Pennsylvania Dutch. ("Dutch" derives from *Deutsch,* meaning German, and does not refer to the language of The Netherlands.) The dialect is the first language Amish children learn, and it was the language spoken by German-speaking immigrants. Second, the Amish learn to read, write, and speak English in school and without interference from their Germanic speech patterns. Third, they acquire a passive knowledge of High German by reading the Bible and by recitation. Their sermons and formal ceremonies are conducted in High German.

When speaking with non-Amish persons they use the English language. An Amish person shifts his conversation between the dialect and English, whichever he finds more appropriate to the occasion.

Because the Amish acquire bilingual competency at an early age, they do not have a noticeable accent. The custom of calling the non-Amish person "English" (the equivalent of outsider, or alien) stems from colonial times when persons were designated by their linguistic community, whether French, Spanish, German, or English. Today its usage does not imply any loyalty to England nor disloyalty to America.

The Rules, Banning, and Shunning

The mission of the church, as the Amish understand it, lies in maintaining a redemptive community. Because the church is to be pure, unspotted, and without blemish (Ephesians 5:27) it must exclude members who live in open sin, those who cause divisions, and those who defy the rules. Twice each year before the observance of the Lord's supper, the members must declare their personal peace and unity with all other members and affirm the discipline. The rules of the Amish church are stated by the ordained leaders and are affirmed anew by each of the members in the congregation.

Punishment for violation of the rules varies with the seriousness of the offense. For a minor infraction of the rules, the violator is rebuked informally by his relatives and neighbors, and eventually by the bishop. For a more serious offense a member is called before a meeting of the members where he is confronted with his offense and given opportunity to amend his ways. Failure to acknowledge wrongdoing results in temporary withdrawal of church privileges. Since the members must give their consent and vote in such disciplinary action, the ordeal is often an emotionally exhausting event. At this stage the offender may, if he does not agree to the rules, migrate to a more liberal Amish community, or leave the Amish faith.

The Amish leaders distinguish between offenses committed in haste or those committed defiantly or deliberately. The threat of shunning is

Children are treasured. Child care and nurture are the most
important adult activities.

a powerful means to prod the individual to conform, for in the Amish church to be shunned has the force of being rejected by God. The most extreme punishment is total excommunication and shunning. Excommunication means exclusion from membership, and shunning requires members no longer to associate with the excommunicated person in social and business relationships. A husband who is shunned is not allowed to eat at the table with his wife, nor sleep in the same bed, nor eat with his own children if they are members. All may admonish him to repent, and provide human needs like food and shelter, but they may not receive favors in return.

This form of shunning was introduced among the Swiss Mennonites by Jacob Ammann in the late seventeenth century. The biblical basis is found in the teaching of Paul (1 Corinthians 5:11) that members should not eat with those who have been excluded from the church nor keep company with them. The Mennonites interpret the teaching to mean that violators should not be admitted to the communion table. The practice of the severe form of shunning (*Meidung*) was the basis on which the Ammann faction separated from the Swiss Mennonites.

Loss of Members

The Amish community is not exempt from deviation and from rebellious individuals. Most offensive to parents are children who deliberately disobey, and most offensive to the church are members who disturb the peace. The Amish emphasize voluntary membership in the church, and there are always a few who choose not to remain faithful. Nevertheless, the Amish have a remarkable record of conformity. Ninety-six percent of the young men who were drafted during World War II were conscientious objectors.

The percentage of young who do not join the church of their parents varies from an estimated 10 to 15 percent from one region to another. Of those who are baptized and later leave the church, the percentage is

This modern family carriage meets safety requirements.
It has battery-operated lights and a red reflector.

much smaller. This loss rate is no threat to the continued existence of the Amish, for their high birthrate assures a steady population growth.

Deviations are of two types: (1) the young who are acquiring adult values and who are testing the boundaries, and (2) those who are lured to the outside. The loss of members is less today than two decades ago. The proliferation of drugs, alienation, loneliness, theft, murder, and the breakdown of the family as portrayed by the media, supports their traditional teaching against worldliness. The Amish are tempted less and less by pleasures in the secular world.

Amish parents exercise patience with their young during the formative years. The young are given full adult work and routine responsibilities on the home and farm, but spiritually they do not acquire adult status until they are baptized. Occasionally a few of the young people's gatherings get out of hand. Barn parties, which include a hired rock band and alcoholic beverages, without the consent or knowledge of the parents, are an embarrassment to the adult community. The parents respect the privacy of their children. Adults do not participate in the gatherings of the young and are careful not to intrude into the activities of their children and friends. Amish parents put up with a lot, believing that patience, manual work, and a strong family will ultimately bring the child around. Experience has proved them right. Most Amish young people change and become steadfast members.

Youth and adults alike may fall prey to alien influences ranging from investment sharks to religious revivals. Those who feel insecure in their personal or religious experience may entertain beliefs which are disruptive to the community. Because the Amish people are not skilled in explaining their religious faith verbally, many are perceived by outsiders as ignorant. The Amish believe that conduct of life and example are more important than words.

One sign of taking on an alien belief is when an Amish person begins to seek "assurance of salvation." This is often set in motion by attendance at prayer services or Bible study groups among churches

A young Amish couple in Sunday dress.

more liberal than the Amish. To assert that one can be sure of going to heaven is to the Amish people a manifestation of boasting. The teaching is disruptive to the community, for it places individual experience above the community. Humility, submissiveness, and hope are the accepted indicators of godliness in waiting for the Great Judgment. Although the Amish accept the fundamental teachings of the Bible, they are not fundamentalists. The differences in religious experience between Amish and other Christian groups are rooted in historical traditions.

Adult Amish persons who seek greater freedom from the discipline will usually join a more liberal Amish, Amish-related, or Mennonite denomination. Assimilation into the dominant culture is usually preceded by verbalization of religious beliefs, interest in evangelism and missionary work, acceptance of automobiles, electricity in the homes, and non-farming occupations.

The Cost of Being Amish

In their early history, the Amish were despised for their heretical beliefs. In America they found religious freedom. Though the persecution has ceased, there are still costs and sacrifices the individual must make for being Amish.

Thieves, some of them in search of antiques, have paid visits to Amish homes. Arsonists have admitted setting fire to Amish barns. In several communities Amish persons have been injured and babies have been killed by rocks thrown at their carriages from speeding automobiles, frequently at night. These acts are sheer devilment on the part of small-town juveniles. Amish schoolchildren have been greeted with jeers and stones by other children when they have migrated into new regions.

The Amish are confronted with regulations and bureaucracies in ways that cause stress and hardships. The long struggle to retain the small schools in their communities, which frequently meant jail sentences for parents and widows, ended with the Supreme Court ruling in 1972. Concerned citizens and friends of the Amish conducted the litigation in their behalf. The Amish oppose compulsory insurance programs. When they did not pay the self-employment old age and survivors insurance tax, the Internal Revenue Service seized their horses to pay the tax. Only after years of harassment were the regulations changed to allow for those with tender conscience.

The Amish appreciate the necessity of government, and they consider rebellion against the state for any reason as unchristian. They pay taxes promptly, but they will not let the state assume the functions of conscience. Some Amish vote in political elections, especially for local officials they know personally. They do not run for public office. They do not go to court to settle disputes among themselves. The use of coercion, whether in a court of law or in personal relationships, is deliberately avoided. Members are admonished to suffer injustices rather than resort to physical force or legal remedies.

Wealth and Class

———

Rumors persist that the Amishman has plenty of hard cash in his pockets and that he can produce it on demand. That popular notion, and the myth that a farmer will paint his gate blue to announce a marriageable daughter, are equally false. The Amish do not keep their money in milk containers but in bank accounts.

The farm income of the Amish farmer is less than that of the average non-Amish farmer. Although he does not have the expense of hiring labor and of maintaining electrical appliances and the high cost of sophisticated farm machinery, an Amish farmer's gross intake is moderate. He does not farm to make money, but to support his family in an environment with minimum interference from the secular world, in a "redemptive community."

Nevertheless, some Amish individuals with substantial wealth are known, both in their own communities and in the nearby trading centers. Ownership of land, hard work, frugality, industry, and honesty are valued, but the strong teaching on sharing, mutual aid, and brotherhood prevent affluent living, competitive spending, and high social standing. A retired Amish farmer may well have bought and paid for several farms in his lifetime. But by outside standards his present income is on a poverty level. The farms were signed over or sold at modest cost to the younger generation. Prestige within the community is measured by how well one works for the good of the community.

Indicators of social class, such as income, education, and symbols of affluence, have no validity in Amish society. There are certain other indicators of prestige, however, based on Amish goals such as obedience, humility, and caring. The highest respect is accorded those couples who are model farmers, who train their children well so that they want to be Amish, and who help the young to settle on farms.

Although there is remarkable homogeneity regarding wealth and spending habits, the Amish rules and customs vary from one region to another. Even within a single community there is variation among families in the orderliness of their farms and their grooming. Well-bred horses, spacious and orderly farm buildings, many varieties of flowers in the house and garden, and decorative china in the corner cupboard are traditional symbols of success. In spite of a high level of homogeneity, some family lines acquire a reputation for industry and others for their lack of it.

The Joys and Satisfactions

The greatest joys in Amish life occur during early childhood and during the mature years. Youth or late adolescence is the most difficult or "dangerous age," when conformity to the rules has the least promise of reward. Nevertheless, the viability of the community is supported by

44

a continuous, consistent pattern of learning and integration. Most Amish persons acquire a sense of who they are, where they have come from, and where they are going.

They are confident, knowing that their basic human needs will be met in a quiet, orderly way. Work, family, mutual aid, religion, and social affirmation, for example, are integrated into a satisfying web of life.

Work is integrated with economic aspirations, for it is through work that the family has food to eat, clothing to wear, and a home to live in. Manual labor on the farm or farm-related crafts have their rewards. Sufficient savings above taxes and expenses to help others in time of need has its own reward. The Amish farmer enjoys his occupation, and unlike the day laborer or factory worker, he can integrate his farm work with the family, with the weather and seasons, and with his own holidays and ceremonial occasions.

Amish families enjoy working with their young and seeing their own values realized in the lives of their children and grandchildren. Every person in the family is needed and useful. By holding labor-saving machines in check, they not only avoid the high cost of machines, but experience the rewards of working together as a family. Such rewards come not only with commitment but with a knowledge of how to teach and be an example to others.

In times of sickness, disaster, or death the support of the community is strong. When a house or barn burns to the ground the Amish provide financial aid, donate their labor, and give strong social support. Not only is there aid in time of disasters, but more routine exchanges of work and services. The women enjoy quiltings, sewings, cleaning, and food-processing activities. The men help each other remodel buildings, paint, butcher, or build fences.

The Amish, in worldly terms, are not pleasure-conscious. But they have their own variety of happiness and gaiety. Many of their normal neighborly activities serve the function of recreation. Couples often travel extensively. The Amish may go fishing, or hunting, and adults frequently take their children to the city zoo. They have small animals for pets. They enjoy the satisfaction of harvest, the simplicity of their home furnishings, orderliness on their farms, and perhaps not least of all, the pleasure of a good meal.

The Amish forgo worldly pleasures in anticipation of eternal life. They live and die in hope of a future reward, but not with the knowledge that they have already attained it.

Although the Amish are communitarian in the sense of caring for and sharing with each other, they are neither a commune nor a model for utopia. Unlike most modern people, they have not rebelled against the restrictions of community, neighborhood, family, and rural village life. The Amish individual has a great deal of freedom (in comparison to many communal groups), though the Amish way of life is not individualistic. The Amish admiration for creation, their respect for nature and order, their practice of personal rather than impersonal relationships, have won the respect of many a visitor. In a world that has grown cold for lack of human contact, traditional communities like the Amish have important lessons to teach us.

Selected References

HISTORY AND CULTURE

Amish Society, John A. Hostetler. Johns Hopkins University Press, Baltimore, Md., 1980.

Our Amish Neighbors, William I. Schreiber. University of Chicago Press, 1962. On the Ohio Amish.

A Peculiar People: Iowa's Old Order Amish, Elmer and Dorothy Schweider. Iowa State University Press, Ames, Iowa, 1975.

PHOTOGRAPHIC STUDIES

The Amish: A Photographic Album, Perry Cragg, Published by Doris Cragg, 1470 Maple Rd., Cleveland, Ohio. Regional study of Ohio Amish.

The Gentle People—A Portrait of the Amish. James Warner and Donald Denlinger. Grossman Publishers, New York. Limited to Lancaster County, Pa.

The Amish: A Pioneer Heritage. John Zielinski, 620 S. Riverside Drive, Iowa City, Iowa. Photos from many regions.

Fields of Peace, A Pennsylvania German Album. Text by Millen Brand. Photos by George A. Tice. Doubleday.

FICTION

Rosanna of the Amish, Joseph W. Yoder. Herald Press, Scottdale, Pa.

Shoo-Fly Girl, Lois Lenski. Lippincott. Juvenile.

Yonie Wondernose, Marguerite de Angeli. Doubleday. For children.

Henner's Lydia, Marguerite de Angeli. Doubleday. For children.

AMISH SCHOOLING

Children in Amish Society, John A. Hostetler and Gertrude E. Huntington. Holt Rinehart Winston, New York, 1967. Case study used in education courses.

Compulsory Education and the Amish, Albert Keim. Beacon Press, Boston, 1975. Discusses the struggle for religious liberty.

COOKBOOKS

Amish Cooking. Pathway Publishers, Lagrange, Indiana.

Wonderful Good Cooking from Amish Country Kitchens, Fred Wilson, et al. Amish Country Publishers, Berlin, Ohio.

QUILTS

A Gallery of Amish Quilts, Robert Bishop and Elizabeth Safanda. E. P. Dutton Co., New York, 1976.

Amish Quilt Designs and Patterns, Phyllis Haders. Main Street Press, Clinton, N.J. 1976.

EDUCATIONAL FILM

The Amish, A People of Preservation. Produced by Heritage Productions, Inc. Two editions: No. 3499, 53 minutes; and No. 3399, 28 minutes. Distributed by Encyclopedia Britannica Educational Corp., 1822 Pickwick Ave., Glenview, Ill. Consult film rental libraries.

THE AUTHOR: John A. Hostetler is Professor of Anthropology and Sociology, Temple University, Philadelphia, Pennsylvania.